ISBN: 9798865331339

All rights reserved. Published by Mary K. Martin.

# WHEN DOGS FLY

## By Mary K. Martin

### Illustrations by Jasmine Kammeyer

Once there was a Missionary Kid
named Ben. A Missionary Kid
is someone whose parents work
in a mission organization,
like Mission Aviation Fellowship (or MAF).

Missionary Kids (or MKs) can live
all over the world, even in faraway
countries like Indonesia, where Ben lived!

Ben lived on an island called Papua, where his dad fixed airplanes to help the MAF pilots fly where help was needed. Back then, there was no internet — not even cellphones! Instead, radios were used to communicate between people. Some places could only be reached by airplanes!

MAF has airplanes throughout Indonesia, and one of the places is Nabire, a tropical beach town. Nabire's airstrip goes right up with the edge of the beach, so airplanes can take off and land right over the ocean! It's a beautiful place to grow up, surrounded by ocean breezes, sand and airplanes.

Ben loved dogs, especially his own dog
— a very good girl named Mattie.

Mattie soon became a momma dog
and raised four healthy puppies.
It was a great time for Ben and his sister
Kara (along with their MAF base friends).

Soon the puppies started to grow,
becoming more and more playful.
But Mattie started to become sicker
and sicker. Something was wrong.
Sadly, Papua didn't have an
animal doctor at the time.

Ben asked his mom, "How can we help Mattie? She is really sick."
His mom explained how she had tried everything she could, but nothing was helping. It looked hopeless.
"Then let's pray," Ben said.

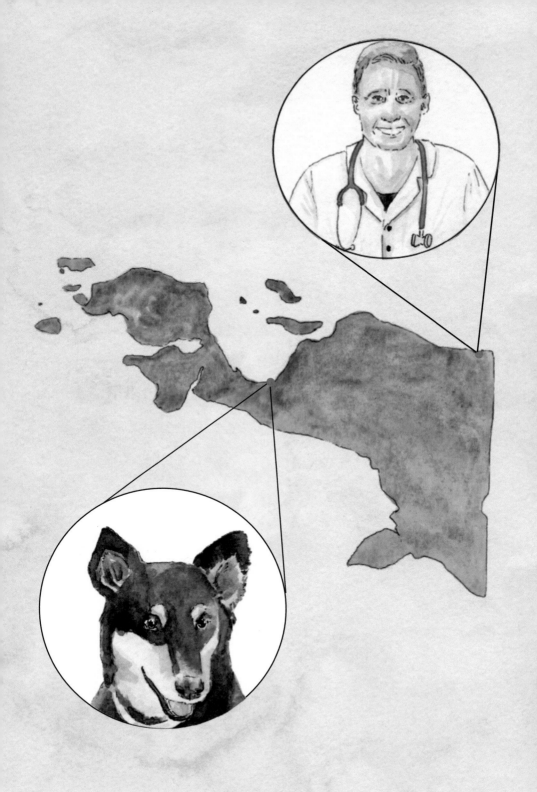

The very hour Ben prayed, his mom
learned by radio there was a visiting
animal doctor willing to care for Mattie —
if she could get to the big city.

Unfortunately, there were no roads from
where they lived to the city, so the only way
to get there was by flying in an airplane.

Amazingly, they found out an MAF plane
was leaving for the big city that morning,
and there was room for Mattie to join the flight!

# LIVE ANIMALS

It was not going to be a fun trip for her.
It would be a very long trip, and she was very sick.
Plus, all animals on her plane would
have to fly below, in the airplane's cargo pod.
(No, not a fun trip at all.)

Ben's Mom radioed ahead and made a plan for Mattie to see the special dog doctor, who was only available for one day. Ben gathered the leash Mattie would need for the flight while his mom collected the medicine the vet needed.

An MAF pilot helped them place Mattie into the cargo pod. The plane landed in the big city a few hours later, and Mattie was rushed to the doctor. He operated on her and was able to heal the infection that had been making Mattie so sick!

The very next day, Mattie flew back home to Nabire. She was groggy, but this time she was allowed to sit inside the plane next to Ben's dad.

Mattie, Ben, and their family had many more good days together at their MAF beach base. Although Mattie never really enjoyed flying after that, she showed them that when they need to, dogs really <u>can</u> fly.

And when dogs fly, it must be because
God's working in a special way.
(A good lesson for Ben and for all of us.)


Hard things help us to grow in our trust and faith
in God. Do you believe God is at work in a special
way in your life? Even when things are hard?


In Luke 18:27, Jesus tells us,
"What is impossible with man is possible with God."

This is a true story about an MAF Missionary Kid.

Ben was only seven years old when he prayed his prayer for Mattie. He spent his childhood growing up in Papua and now works as an aircraft mechanic (just like his Dad!) and has a family of his own.

And, of course, he has a great dog — a very good boy named Grizzly. (Ben's pretty sure Grizzly can fly if he needs to....)

Illustrator Jasmine Kammeyer lived in Nabire with her family from 2000 to 2004, while her Dad was a pilot for MAF.

Currently she is a Vet Tech and artist with a family of her own — and a very good dog named Nala.

# Think about ways to find help in hard times...

In the Bible, the writer James tells us "if any of you lacks wisdom, you should ask God, who gives generously to all without finding fault and it will be given to you." (James 1:5) Asking God to help us when we face hard things is important. God will help us find wise solutions to our problems.

Are there hard things in your life that you
want to ask God to help you with today?
Feel free to write about it below.

# Think about prayer...

Praying is talking to God. It can be a chance
to ask for help or to thank Him for all the
good things He's given you in your life.
It's okay to write down your prayers, too.

Do you have a prayer you would
like to make to God today?

# Think about getting help for any worries...

In Matthew 11:28, Jesus said, "Come to me, all you who are weary and burdened, and I will give you rest." In Ben's story, a prayer for help brought immediate relief to a worried dog owner, and his pet received the help she needed.

Do you have any worries
or concerns in your life today?

Maybe now is a good time
to talk with God about it and write
down your thoughts or feelings.

Papua is a remote part of Indonesia, and Nabire can be located on its northern coast.

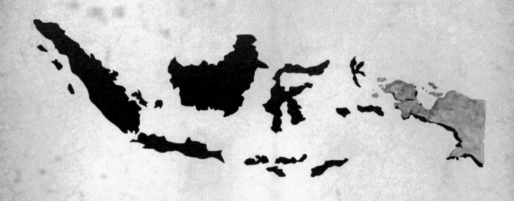

In Papua there are five bases of operation, with 9 airplanes serving the people there.

Nabire base was built on the oceanfront in 1955 and was called "The Jungle Gateway."

Today the planes from Nabire fly to help many villages on the western part of Papua.

MAF Vision Statement

To see isolated people changed by the love of Christ.

MAF Mission Statement

Serving together to bring help, hope,
and healing through aviation.

And on rare occasions, when
an airplane's pod is empty and God arranges it,
a Missionary Kid's dog can fly, too.

Made in United States
Troutdale, OR
02/15/2024